Come Camping

By Jill Atkins

Published in 2026 by
Norwood House Press
2544 Clinton Street
Buffalo, NY 14224

Printed in the United States of America

Library of Congress Cataloging-in-Publication Data:
Names: Atkins, Jill (Children's author).
Title: Come camping ; Karting / written by Jill Atkins.
Description: Buffalo, NY : Norwood House Press, 2026. | Series: Phonics all-stars: phase 4
Identifiers: ISBN 9781978578203 (pbk.) | ISBN 9781978578210 (library bound) | ISBN 9781978578227 (ebook)
Subjects: LCSH: Reading–Phonetic method–Juvenile fiction. | English language–Phonetics–Juvenile fiction. | Camping–Juvenile fiction. | Karting–Juvenile fiction.
Classification: LCC LB1573.3 A796 2026 | DDC 372.465–dc23

CPSIA compliance information: Batch #CW26NHP: For further information contact Norwood House Press at 1-800-237-9932.

If you are fond of fresh air and fun, come with us on a camping trip.

You will need to bring a
tent and a sleeping bag.

You might bring some pots and pans, forks, spoons and mugs too.

You will need a flashlight or a lamp for dark nights.

Pick a good spot for the tent.

Fix it well with tent pegs.

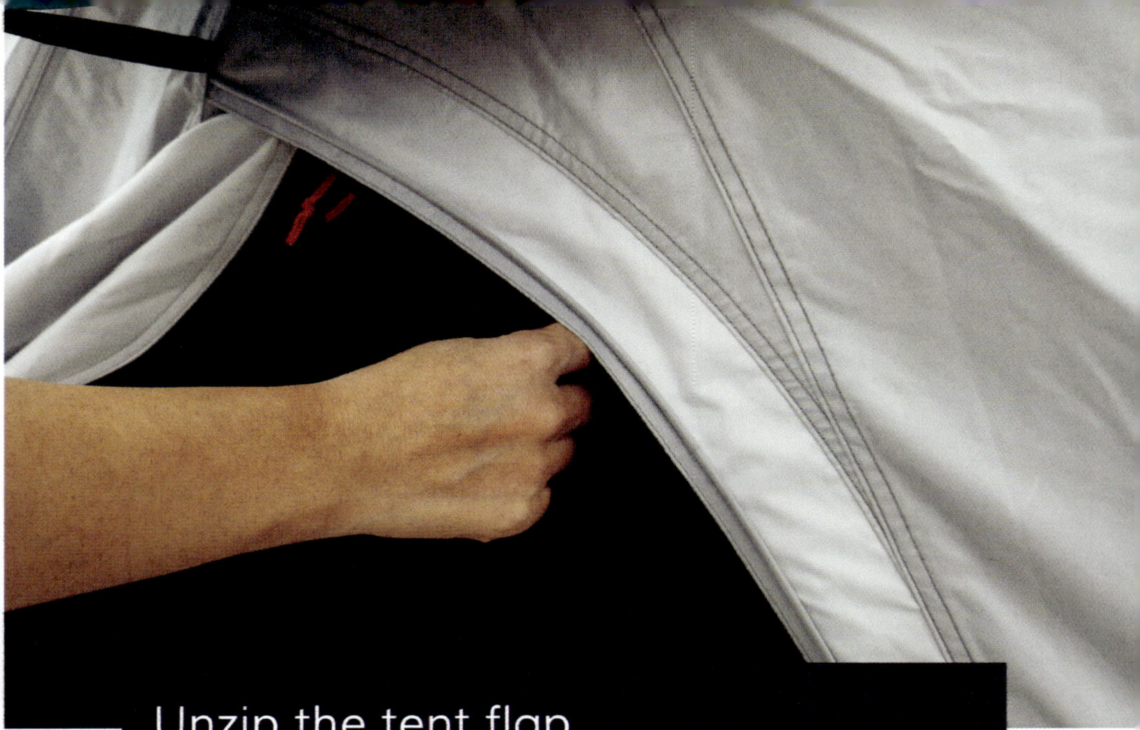

Unzip the tent flap.

In you go!

Good night. See you in the morning.

On a clear night, you will see loads of stars.

If you camp on a farm, some sheep or cows might come near you.

If you camp near the coast, you might go for a swim.

Or you might go surfing.

Now you need some food.

To start, pick up some wood so you can cook some fish.

It will smell terrific, but you must not let the fish burn!

It is fun to stick sweets on the end of a twig.

They melt as they get hot.

Yum!

Is camping fun? Or is it just grim food, wet tents and too much mess?

You tell me!

Go-Karting

By Jill Atkins

Were you looking for a fun sport to do?

Well, you might have a crack at go-karting.

There might be a track near you.

Go there if you can.

Go-karting is the sort of thing you can do just for fun.

Or you can train and get some better skills.

Then you might turn into the best!

You will need all the gear.

This might all cost a lot, but you can rent this stuff with a go-kart.

Do not forget the helmet.

6

Some go-karts have a bar at the back, to stop you getting hurt if you flip.

Some go-karts have a lot of power and are quick.

Go-karts for teens and kids have less power. This is so that they do not crash the kart on the track.

You have to plug some go-karts in to get power.

This plug-in kart is terrific. Is it a hot rod?

A lot of top car champs were in go-karts as kids.

Some of them were go-kart champs then, and are car champs now.

Will she be a champ too?